AF599318

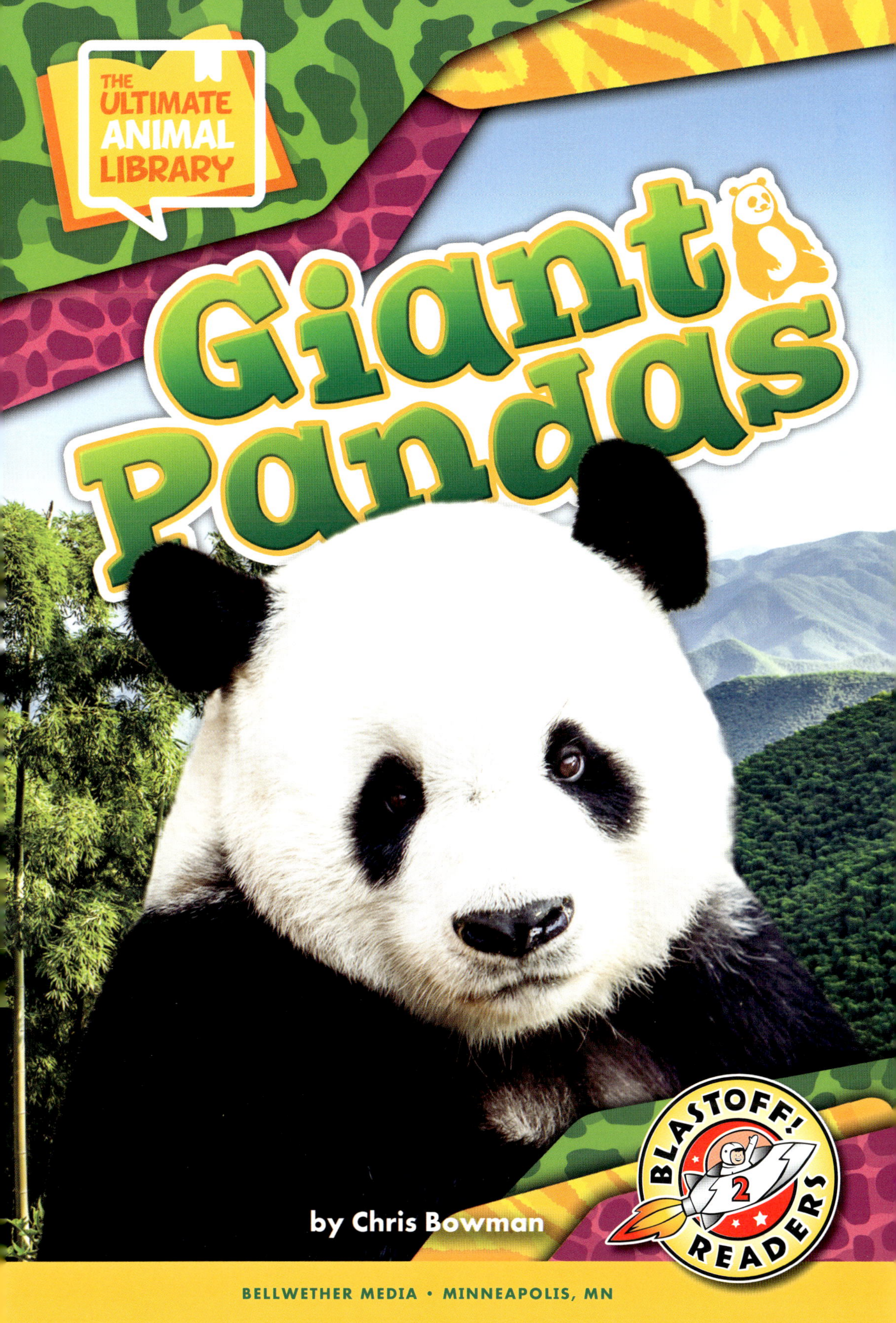
THE ULTIMATE ANIMAL LIBRARY
Giant Pandas
by Chris Bowman
BLASTOFF! READERS
2
BELLWETHER MEDIA • MINNEAPOLIS, MN

Blastoff! Readers are carefully developed by literacy experts to build reading stamina and move students toward fluency by combining standards-based content with developmentally appropriate text.

Level 1 provides the most support through repetition of high-frequency words, light text, predictable sentence patterns, and strong visual support.

Level 2 offers early readers a bit more challenge through varied sentences, increased text load, and text-supportive special features.

Level 3 advances early-fluent readers toward fluency through increased text load, less reliance on photos, advancing concepts, longer sentences, and more complex special features.

★ **Blastoff! Universe**

Reading Level

This edition first published in 2025 by Bellwether Media, Inc.

Library of Congress Cataloging-in-Publication Data

LC record for Giant Pandas available at: https://lccn.loc.gov/2024012113

Editor: Elizabeth Neuenfeldt Series Designer: Veah Demmin

Printed in the United States of America, North Mankato, MN.

Table of Contents

What Are Giant Pandas?

Giant pandas are large **mammals**. They are members of the bear family. They are only found in China.

Giant Panda Report

range =

Status in the Wild

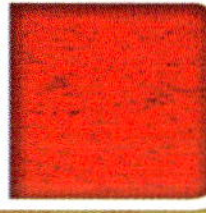

vulnerable

Habitat

mountain forests

Pandas have big bodies. They can grow to about 5 feet (1.5 meters) long.

Some weigh up to 300 pounds (136 kilograms)!

Giant pandas have large heads and short, rounded ears.

They have strong teeth and jaws to eat bamboo.

Pandas have white heads with black ears and black marks around their eyes. Their bodies are white with black legs.

Their thick fur helps them stay warm.

Spot a Giant Panda
big head
large body
white body with black legs

Big Eaters

Giant pandas live high up in mountain forests.

They like to be in
cool **temperatures**.
They usually live alone.

Pandas mostly walk on four legs. They are also strong climbers and swimmers.

Males sometimes do handstands. This helps them mark their **territory** with their **scent**.

Pandas mainly eat bamboo. They hold it with a special bone in their front paws.

Pandas spend around 12 hours per day eating!

Growing Up

Female giant pandas give birth to one or two **cubs**. They give birth around every two years.

Newborn cubs are small and all white. Their eyes open after about two months.

cub

Panda cubs play with mom.
Mom keeps cubs safe
from **predators**.

Cubs **nurse** for up to two years. Then they live on their own. Time to find bamboo!

Life of a Giant Panda

Name of Babies

Number of Babies

Time Spent with Mom

Life Span

Glossary

cubs—baby giant pandas

mammals—warm-blooded animals that have backbones and feed their young milk

newborn—just recently born

nurse—to drink mom's milk

predators—animals that hunt other animals for food

scent—a smell or odor

temperatures—measurements of heat and cold

territory—a land area where an animal lives

To Learn More

AT THE LIBRARY

Davies, Monika. *China.* Minneapolis, Minn.: Bellwether Media, 2023.

Grack, Rachel. *Giant Pandas.* Minneapolis, Minn.: Bellwether Media, 2022.

Markarian, Margie. *Pandas.* Washington, D.C.: National Geographic, 2021.

ON THE WEB

FACTSURFER

Factsurfer.com gives you a safe, fun way to find more information.

1. Go to www.factsurfer.com.
2. Enter "giant pandas" into the search box and click 🔍.
3. Select your book cover to see a list of related content.

Index

The images in this book are reproduced through the courtesy of: InnaPoka, series patterns; 06photo, cover background, interior background; Creativa Images, cover (giant panda); Denis Sarbashev, cover (panda icon); Eric Isselee, pp. 3, 23; Fernan Archilla, p. 4; clkarus, pp. 6, 10-11, 17 (panda); Wonderly Imaging, pp. 7, 12; asharkyu, p. 8; Bryan Faust, p. 9; ex0rzist, p. 10; chuyuss, p. 11; Keren Su/China Span/ Alamy, p. 13; oversnap, p. 14; Nature Picture Library/ Alamy, p. 15; Foreverhappy-Mee, pp. 16-17; Boxun Liu, p. 17 (bamboo); Steve Bloom Images/ Alamy, p. 18; Corbin17/ Alamy, pp. 18-19; ZSSD/Minden Pictures, p. 20; Foreverhappy, p. 21.